REMARKABLE CANADIANS

Elijah Harper

by Rebecca Szulhan

Published by Weigl Educational Publishers Limited
6325 – 10 Street SE
Calgary, Alberta, Canada
T2H 2Z9

Website: www.weigl.com

Library and Archives Canada Cataloguing in Publication

Szulhan, Rebecca
        Elijah Harper / Rebecca Szulhan.
(Remarkable Canadians)
Includes index.
ISBN 978-1-55388-309-8 (bound).--ISBN 978-1-55388-310-4 (pbk.)
                        1. Harper, Elijah, 1949- --Juvenile literature.
2. Cabinet ministers--Manitoba--Biography--Juvenile literature.
3. Politicians--Manitoba--Biography--Juvenile literature.
4. Cree Indians--Biography--Juvenile literature.
5. Legislators--Canada--Biography--Juvenile literature.
6. Canada. Parliament. House of Commons--Biography--
Juvenile literature. I. Title. II. Series.

FC3377.1.H37S98 2007   j971.27'03092   C2007-900888-7

Printed in the United States of America
1 2 3 4 5 6 7 8 9 0 11 10 09 08 07

Editor: Liz Brown
Design: Terry Paulhus

We acknowledge the financial support of the Government of Canada through the Book
Publishing Industry Development Program (BPIDP) for our publishing activities.

Cover: Elijah Harper is a well-known First Nations leader.

Photograph Credits
Cover: CP (Wayne Glowacki); Assembly of First Nations: page 13 (all photos); CP:
pages 9 (Ken Gigliotti), 10 (Wayne Glowacki), 14 (Gerry Cairns), 18 (Wayne
Glowacki), 20 (John Hyrniuk); Courtesy of Elijah Harper: pages 5, 6, 15, 17, 19;
Province of Manitoba: page 7 top left.

Contents

Who Is Elijah Harper?

Elijah Harper is best known for his work as a **politician**. In the 1970s, Elijah was chief of the Red Sucker Lake First Nation, in northern Manitoba. In 1981, he was elected to the Manitoba **legislative assembly**. This was the first time a **treaty First Nations** person had become a member of a provincial legislative assembly. Elijah is well known for opposing the **Meech Lake Accord**. He felt the issues of Aboriginal Peoples were being ignored in the accord. Elijah has been an **advocate** for Aboriginal Peoples for many years. He teaches people about Aboriginal **cultures**. Although Elijah is no longer an elected member of government, he continues to promote Aboriginal rights.

> "I guess I figured that as politicians and as government you could change things."

Growing Up

Elijah was born on March 3, 1949, on the Red Sucker Lake **reserve** in northern Manitoba. He is one of 13 children born to Allan and Ethel Harper. Elijah's **ancestors** were Cree and Ojibwa. These are two First Nations groups.

Elijah grew up in Red Sucker Lake. He was raised by his grandparents, John E. Harper and Juliette Harper. They taught him about his **heritage**. Elijah saw his parents and siblings every day. He also enjoyed visiting his other relatives.

In 1954, Elijah became sick. A doctor decided that he needed to be sent to a hospital. Later, Elijah stayed at a **tuberculosis sanatorium**. He was only five years old. Elijah was sent home when he began feeling better. His family was happy to see him. Elijah had been gone for six months.

🍁 Elijah (top left) is the second-oldest sibling in his family.

Manitoba Tidbits

COAT OF ARMS

TREE White Spruce

FLOWER Prairie Crocus

The great grey owl is Manitoba's provincial bird.

Aboriginal Peoples farmed along the Red River in Manitoba as early as AD 1100.

When the province was created, it was much smaller than it is today. Manitoba was called the "postage stamp" province because it was so small.

The name Manitoba comes from the Cree word "Manitou," which means "Great Spirit."

Winnipeg is the provincial capital.

Think about it!

Manitoba is the province where Elijah Harper was born. Research the province's history. Learn about the people living in Manitoba today. How might these factors have influenced Elijah to become a politician?

Practice Makes Perfect

Elijah learned many things from his grandparents. They taught him about their culture and ancestors. Elijah also learned many lessons from his own experiences growing up on a reserve. He understood the challenges Aboriginal Peoples faced.

Elijah attended high school in Garden Hill, Manitoba, and at the Winnipeg Dakota Collegiate, in Winnipeg. He enrolled as a student at the University of Manitoba in 1971. Elijah joined a group that helped other Aboriginal students. If Aboriginal students had problems or concerns, the group helped them find solutions.

🍁 The University of Manitoba is located in Winnipeg.

Elijah took a job with the Manitoba Department of Northern Affairs in 1975. He met many politicians and learned how the government worked. Elijah learned that through politics, he could make a difference. In 1978, he resigned from his job. Later that year, Elijah was elected chief of Red Sucker Lake. He remained chief until 1981.

Elijah was elected to be a member of the legislative assembly of Manitoba in 1981. He held this position until 1992. In 1993, Elijah ran in the **federal** election. He was elected to be a member of the House of Commons in Ottawa. Elijah was appointed Commissioner of the Indian Claims Commission in 1999. In this job, he helped First Nations peoples work with the government to settle disputes.

🍁 Elijah spoke in Cree and English during his first speech in the Manitoba legislative assembly.

Key Events

In 1982, Elijah gave his first speech as a member of the legislative assembly. Elijah spoke about the needs and wants of Aboriginal Peoples in Canada.

In 1990, Elijah opposed the Meech Lake Accord. The Meech Lake Accord was an agreement between the **premiers** of all the provinces to recognize Quebec as a **distinct** society. This agreement was first discussed in 1987. It was named after Meech Lake, Quebec, where the meeting took place.

Elijah and other Aboriginal Peoples felt that their rights had been ignored in this agreement. They had not been included in the discussions about the Meech Lake Accord.

In a speech, Elijah told the Manitoba Legislature that he would not accept the accord. Both the Manitoba and Newfoundland governments did not vote on the accord.

🦅 Elijah held an eagle feather in his hand while he spoke about the Meech Lake Accord. The eagle feather is a symbol of spiritual strength for First Nations peoples.

Thoughts from Elijah

Elijah became a politician to make people aware of the rights and needs of Canada's Aboriginal Peoples. Here are some things he has said about his life and career.

Elijah talks about Aboriginal beliefs.

"Everything is a living thing; the water, the land."

Elijah talks about the lessons he learned from his grandparents.

"It was a very important part of my life, part of my culture and heritage to adopt and instill in me the values of my people. It is very important because your identity is instilled in you when you are very young."

Elijah talks about how his stand against the Meech Lake Accord helped many people.

"Many people have come and said to me, 'Thank you for the stand you took' — not just Aboriginal people but many ordinary Canadians."

Elijah explains why he and other Aboriginal Peoples were upset with the Meech Lake Accord.

"We're saying that Aboriginal issues should be put on the priority list."

Elijah talks about the ways that Aboriginal rights have been ignored.

"I never heard my dad, or grandfather, or anyone, talk about voting, because they weren't allowed to vote."

Elijah makes his first speech in the Manitoba Legislature.

"I am glad that you have elected me. I say that to you all."

What Is a Politician?

Elijah worked as a politician at the provincial level and at the federal level. As a member of Manitoba's legislative assembly, he represented his **constituency** within the province. When he was elected to the House of Commons, he represented his constituency to other Canadians.

There is a legislative assembly in each province and territory. In Quebec, it is called the national assembly. Legislative and national assemblies make laws that apply to the areas they represent. A person who is elected to work in the legislative assembly is called a Member of the Legislative Assembly (MLA).

The House of Commons also has elected members. Members of the House of Commons are called Members of Parliament (MP). Members of Parliament make laws that affect all of Canada. There are 308 Members of Parliament.

❧ The House of Commons is located in Ottawa, Canada's capital city.

Politicians 101

Phil Fontaine (1944–)

Phil Fontaine is from Manitoba. He is currently the National Chief of the Assembly of First Nations. This is Fontaine's second term as National Chief. He was first elected in 1997. Fontaine has spoken publicly about his experiences at **residential schools**. He has brought attention to the experiences Aboriginal students had at these schools.

Awards: Member of the Order of Manitoba, 2003.

Georges Erasmus (1948–)

Georges Erasmus was born in Fort Rae, Northwest Territories. He is a member of the Dene group of First Nations. Erasmus supported the Dene Declaration. This document was created in 1975 to outline the rights of the Dene people. Erasmus was the president of the Indian Brotherhood of Northwest Territories. In 1985, he became National Chief of the Assembly of First Nations. Erasmus served as National Chief until 1991.

Awards: Member of the Order of Canada, 1987; Officer of the Order of Canada, 1989.

Matthew Coon Come (1956–)

In 1981, Matthew Coon Come became chief of the Mistissini Cree. He held this position until 1986. In 1992, Coon Come helped stop the Quebec government from building a **hydro-electric** project in northern Quebec. This project would have damaged an area of wilderness the size of France. Coon Come became National Chief of the Assembly of First Nations in 2000.

Awards: Equinox Environmental Prize, 1993; The Goldman Environmental Prize, 1994.

Walter Dieter (1916–1918)

Walter Dieter was born in Saskatchewan. He was Cree and a member of the Peepeekisis Band. Dieter helped create the National Indian Brotherhood in 1969. He also helped create the Assembly of First Nations. Dieter was the first National Chief of the Assembly of First Nations.

Awards: Officer of the Order of Canada, 1980.

Assembly of First Nations

The Assembly of First Nations is a national organization. The group represents the needs, wants, and concerns of First Nations in Canada. The Assembly of First Nations is headed by a National Chief. The National Chief is chosen through an election. All of the Chiefs of the Assembly vote to decide who will be the next National Chief. They meet throughout the year to plan activities and discuss policies. The National Chief serves for three years.

Influences

Many people influenced Elijah. Elijah's family has always been important to him. From his family, Elijah learned about his heritage. When Elijah began working, he met people who helped his career. They taught him how to be a politician.

Elijah was raised by his grandparents. Elijah's grandparents taught him to appreciate his culture. He learned to speak the Cree language when he was a child. Elijah also learned to hunt, fish, and canoe when he was young.

🍁 Elijah (front left) has helped teach other Canadians about First Nations problems through marches and peaceful protests.

In 1975, Elijah took a job as a **program analyst** with the Manitoba Department of Northern Affairs. While working at this job, he met politicians such as Edward Schreyer, who was the premier of Manitoba at the time. Elijah enjoyed his job. The politicians that Elijah met taught him how the government worked.

In 1981, Elijah decided to **campaign** for a position in the Manitoba legislative assembly. As an elected official, Elijah wanted to teach people about the problems facing Aboriginal Peoples. He also wanted to teach them about the contributions Aboriginal Peoples had made to Canada.

RED SUCKER LAKE

Elijah was influenced by his childhood at Red Sucker Lake. Elijah's community traded with the Hudson's Bay Company. The trading brought new technologies to Aboriginal communities. Airplanes and boats brought mail and supplies. Some traditional Cree activities began to change. When Elijah was a child, Aboriginal Peoples were not allowed to vote in federal elections. When Elijah became a politician, he tried to help Aboriginal Peoples and non-Aboriginal Peoples understand each other.

🍁 Red Sucker Lake is a small community with a population of around 800 people.

Overcoming Obstacles

Elijah has faced several obstacles in his career. Sometimes, people have not liked his decisions. He learned how to overcome these obstacles. Elijah did not let these problems stop him from achieving success.

Elijah worked as a member of the Manitoba legislative assembly in Winnipeg. Life in Winnipeg was different from life in Red Sucker Lake. Hunting was important to Elijah and the other people in Red Sucker Lake. In Winnipeg, Elijah's job as a member of the Manitoba legislative assembly was very important. He had to attend many meetings.

🍁 Moose is one animal that Elijah hunts. Each fall, Elijah spends time camping in the forest to hunt moose.

Once, Elijah missed a meeting without telling anyone he would not be there. His coworkers became worried about him. When they were able to contact him, Elijah told them that he was on a hunting trip. Elijah's coworkers did not understand why Elijah had left work to hunt. This was because hunting was not important in their culture. Elijah and his coworkers worked hard to understand each other's lifestyles.

Elijah served as a Member of Parliament when Jean Chrétien was prime minister of Canada. When Elijah was welcomed into parliament, he brought his father to meet Jean Chrétien.

Achievements and Successes

Elijah has had much success in his career as a politician. He taught people about Aboriginal culture and its importance to Canada. As a politician, Elijah worked hard to protect Aboriginal Peoples' rights.

Elijah was voted newsmaker of the year by the Canadian Press in 1990. This was in recognition of his role in the Meech Lake Accord debates. In 1996, Elijah was awarded a National Aboriginal Achievement Award in public service. This recognized his dedication to helping solve the problems that Aboriginal Peoples face.

Elijah encourages Aboriginal Peoples to be proud of their heritage. He urges all Aboriginal Peoples and non-Aboriginal peoples to understand each other.

During the Meech Lake Accord discussions, many people gathered outside the Manitoba legislature to support Elijah's position.

Elijah brought Aboriginal Peoples and non-Aboriginal peoples together for a meeting in Hull, Quebec, in 1995. This meeting was called the Sacred Assembly. Elders and leaders from both groups talked about their concerns for their people. Elijah arranged the meeting so that the two groups could learn more about each other.

Another Sacred Assembly was held in 1997 at the Sagkeeng First Nation in Manitoba. At these meetings, Canadian leaders talked about the problems facing Canada's Aboriginal Peoples. They agreed to work together to find solutions to these problems.

ELIJAH'S WORK OUTSIDE CANADA

Elijah has travelled to other countries for meetings. In Taiwan, he attended the conference on the Lifestyles of Aboriginal Children Around the World. Elijah met many people from around the world. It was a chance for people to share their experiences. Different cultures met and talked. They shared ideas and formed relationships. At these meetings, Elijah talked about Canadian Aboriginal Peoples.

🍁 Elijah's family has been with him for many important moments in his career.

Write a Biography

A person's life story can be the subject of a book. This kind of book is called a biography. Biographies describe the lives of remarkable people, such as those who have achieved great success or have done important things to help others. These people may be alive today, or they may have lived many years ago. Reading a biography can help you learn more about a remarkable person.

At school, you might be asked to write a biography. First, decide who you want to write about. You can choose a politician, such as Elijah Harper, or any other person you find interesting. Then, find out if your library has any books about this person. Learn as much as you can about him or her. Write down the key events in this person's life. What was this person's childhood like? What has he or she accomplished? What are his or her goals? What makes this person special or unusual?

A concept web is a useful research tool. Read the questions in the following concept web. Answer the questions in your notebook. Your answers will help you write your biography.

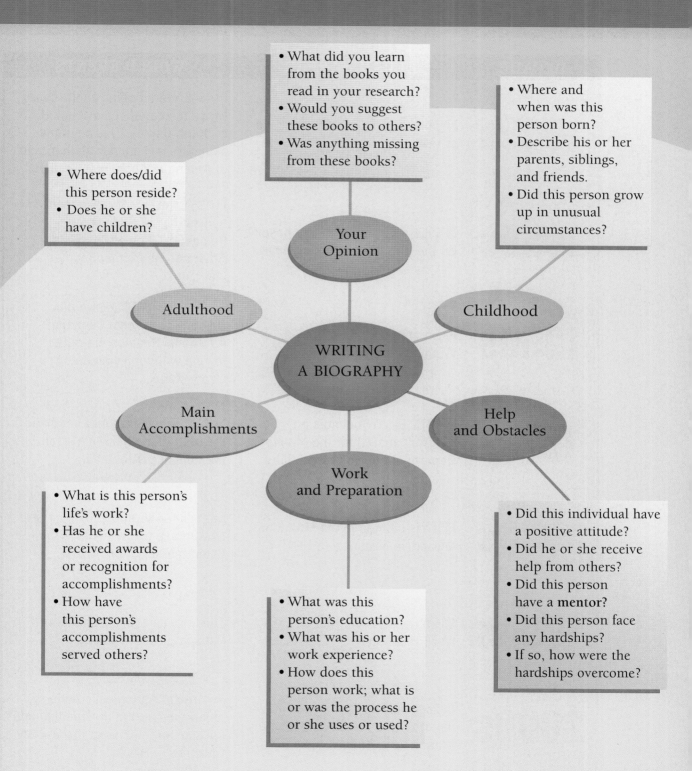

- What did you learn from the books you read in your research?
- Would you suggest these books to others?
- Was anything missing from these books?

- Where and when was this person born?
- Describe his or her parents, siblings, and friends.
- Did this person grow up in unusual circumstances?

- Where does/did this person reside?
- Does he or she have children?

Your Opinion

Adulthood

Childhood

WRITING A BIOGRAPHY

Main Accomplishments

Help and Obstacles

Work and Preparation

- What is this person's life's work?
- Has he or she received awards or recognition for accomplishments?
- How have this person's accomplishments served others?

- Did this individual have a positive attitude?
- Did he or she receive help from others?
- Did this person have a **mentor**?
- Did this person face any hardships?
- If so, how were the hardships overcome?

- What was this person's education?
- What was his or her work experience?
- How does this person work; what is or was the process he or she uses or used?

Timeline

DECADE	ELIJAH HARPER	WORLD EVENTS
1940s	Elijah is born at Red Sucker Lake in 1949.	In 1948, work begins on the Crazy Horse memorial in the Black Hills of South Dakota. This mountain sculpture will honour the heritage of American Aboriginal Peoples.
1950s	In 1954, Elijah is taken to a hospital for the treatment of tuberculosis.	In 1952, the U.S. government begins the Urban Indian Relocation Program to move American Aboriginal Peoples into cities.
1960s	Elijah attends high school in Winnipeg and Garden Hill.	In 1960, Prime Minister John Diefenbaker grants Canadian Aboriginal Peoples the right to vote without giving up treaty status.
1970s	In 1975, Elijah becomes a program analyst for the Manitoba Department of Northern Affairs.	In 1971, Neville Bonner becomes the first Aboriginal Member of Parliament in Australia.
1980s	Elijah is elected to the Manitoba legislative assembly in 1981.	Canadian Aboriginal Peoples are guaranteed treaty rights in the **Constitution** Act of 1982.
1990s	Elijah opposes the Meech Lake Accord in 1990.	The last residential school in Canada closes in 1996.
2000s	In 2006, filming begins on a movie about Elijah's role in defeating the Meech Lake Accord.	Australian Aboriginal culture is celebrated during the opening and closing ceremonies at the Sydney Olympics in 2000.

Further Research

How can I find out more about Elijah Harper?

Most libraries have computers that connect to a database for researching information. If you input a key word, you will be provided with a list of books in the library that contain information on that topic. Non-fiction books are arranged numerically, using their call number. Fiction books are organized alphabetically by the author's last name.

Websites

To learn more about Elijah Harper, visit
www.nationmedia.ca/elijahharper

To learn more about the Meech Lake Accord, go to
www.histori.ca, and type "Meech Lake Accord" into
the search engine.

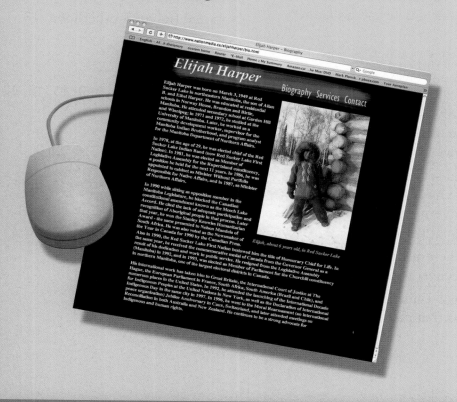

Words to Know

advocate: a person who defends the interests of other people or things

ancestors: relatives from a long time ago

campaign: to solicit votes for an election

constituency: a group of voters in a certain area

Constitution: laws of Canada

cultures: the beliefs and customs of different groups of people

distinct: different from others

federal: level of government for all of Canada

First Nations: indigenous people of Canada who are not Inuit or Métis

heritage: someone or something's history

hydro-electric: electricity generated using flowing water

legislative assembly: the place where provincial laws are passed

Meech Lake Accord: an agreement between the provinces to recognize Quebec as a distinct society in Canada.

mentor: a wise and trusted teacher

politician: a person who is elected to work in the government

premiers: leaders of provincial governments

program analyst: someone who studies government activities for his or her job

reserve: an area of land set aside by the government for use by Aboriginal Peoples

residential schools: government sponsored schools for Aboriginal Peoples

sanatorium: a place where people who are ill go to rest and recover

treaty: official status as a Canadian Aboriginal

tuberculosis: an illness that causes problems in the lungs

Index